Eighteen Sixty One

plus four means

President Lincoln

and

Civil War

1 8 6 1

YEAR OF
LINCOLN
1861

by Genevieve Foster

Charles Scribner's Sons   New York

CONTENTS

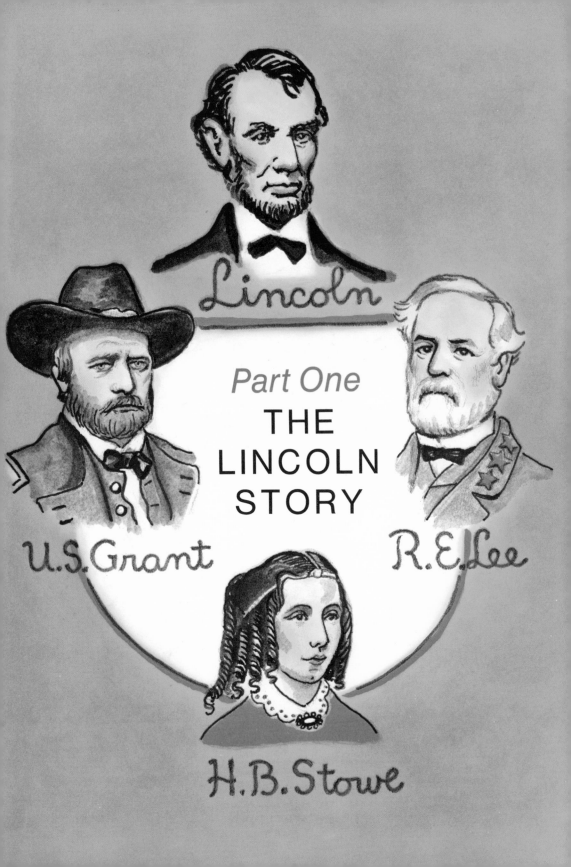

Lincoln

Part One

THE
LINCOLN
STORY

U.S. Grant

R.E. Lee

H.B. Stowe

SPRINGFIELD ILLINOIS

O N FEBRUARY 11, 1861, the day before his fifty-
second birthday, Abraham Lincoln was leaving his
home in Springfield, Illinois, for Washington, D.C., to become the sixteenth President of the United States.

7

1861

It was a cold, drizzly morning. Smoke from the funnel-shaped stack of the small engine hung low over the crowd at the railroad station. In his high black hat and with a shawl about his shoulders, Lincoln shook hands with everyone he could reach before boarding the train.

Mrs. Lincoln and the three boys were with him. Robert, eighteen, was going east to enter Harvard College. William, who was eleven, and Tad, who was eight, were excited about the train ride. Soon Lincoln appeared alone on the back platform. As he stood there looking out upon all those friendly faces, he spoke these words of farewell:

"My friends, no one can appreciate my feeling of sadness at this parting. To this place and the kindness of these people I owe everything. Here I have lived for a quarter of a century and passed from a young man to an old. I now leave not knowing when or whether I may return, with a task before me greater than that which rested on Washington. Trusting in Him who can go with me and remain with you, let us confidently hope that all will be well."

The train whistled. It began to move. The tall, dark figure on the platform grew smaller and smaller and was gone. Those who watched would never see him again.

The country was in an uproar. Southern Democrats were furious that what they called a "black Republican" had been elected President. They threatened to break away from the Union if he lived to take the oath of office. Friends in New York and other cities of the East feared he might never reach the capital. Many letters had come to Lincoln from people threatening to kill him if he dared to leave Springfield for Washington.

A few weeks before he left, Lincoln had gone "down state" to see an old lady whom he always called the best friend he ever had, his dear, good stepmother, Sarah Bush Lincoln. His father, Thomas, was dead, but his stepmother was still living in the old log cabin which Abe had helped build for them thirty years ago. After the cabin was built, he had plowed the new land, put in the first crops, and split rails for the zigzag fences that marked off the fields. Then he had left home to make his own way in the world with no idea of what he could do or what he would become.

The story of President Lincoln and the Civil War really begins in 1830. In that year the Lincoln family were moving to Illinois and Andrew Jackson was President of the United States.

IN 1830, ABRAHAM LINCOLN was twenty-one years
old. He had been born in Kentucky and lived there until he
was seven. Then his easygoing father took a notion to move
across the Ohio River to the woods of Indiana where the hunting was better. In February, 1830, the Lincolns and their
kinfolk were moving to the prairies of Illinois, where they
had heard farming was easier and hunting just as good.

Abe walked all the way to Illinois, plodding along beside
the oxen as the covered wagon lumbered on through the
half-frozen mud and slush. Now and then he told a funny

10

1830

story or joke to keep the rest of the family cheered up. Most of the time he was thinking about something he had read in the newspaper just before they started and wondering what President Jackson would say about it.

There had been a hot debate in Congress between a senator from South Carolina and a senator from Massachusetts over whether or not any state had the right to disobey a law passed by the United States government.

The senator from South Carolina objected to a law that Congress had passed, which he said was good for the factory owners of Massachusetts but bad for the plantation owners of South Carolina. And the state intended to disobey it. What's more, it had a perfect right to do so.

"Nonsense," replied the senator from Massachusetts. "If every state in the Union could disobey any law it wanted to, soon there would be no United States."

For a time President Andrew Jackson did not express his opinion. But when South Carolina threatened to withdraw

11

from the Union unless the law was done away with, his eyes flashed and this is what he said:

"No state has a right to secede from the Union. That is treason. Our Federal Union must be preserved."

Andrew Jackson was a fighter, ready to settle that question then and there, without bloodshed, if possible, but at any price. He was prevented from doing so by a soft-spoken senator from Kentucky, who could always find some way to smooth over an argument. Now he suggested that the law to which South Carolina objected should be done away with—not all at once, but gradually. So the argument was stopped, but the question remained unsettled.

Did any state have the right to secede from the Union?

Thirty years later that question would have to be answered, and the one to do it would be the young man plodding along beside the ox team on his way to Illinois.

THIS IS A MAP OF THE UNITED STATES in 1830, when there were only twenty-four states. These were divided into twelve states where black people were held as slaves and twelve states where they were free. The Ohio River formed the dividing line.

Territories

UNITED STATES — 1830

▭ Free States   ▨ Slave States

▨ Territories

L. Lincoln's Birthplace   C. Cincinnati
S. Springfield   W. Washington, D.C.

The rest of the country was spaced off into large territories. As soon as there were enough settlers living in any part of a territory, it could become a state. As new states were added, Congress kept the number equal by adding one slave state and one free state at the same time.

However, in 1830 people in the free states were saying that there should be no more slave states. Some declared that even where it now existed slavery should be done away with. Many who lived along the Ohio River helped runaway slaves get across the river and escape.

They also set up a system whereby these runaway slaves were hidden in various places and smuggled on from one place to another until they felt safe. Some traveled in this way as far as Canada. The system was so secret and swift it was called the Underground Railroad.

Some of the slaves who escaped did whatever they could to help others. One of these was Harriet Tubman, who helped over three hundred black people to find their way to freedom. She liked to call herself a "conductor" on the Underground Railroad and always took pride in saying that she had never lost a "passenger."

Between 1830 and 1850 about 40,000 slaves had escaped.

During those years six new states had been added—three slave and three free. So far Congress had managed to keep the number equal. But in 1850 there was trouble.

California asked to be admitted as a free state. The senator from South Carolina objected because, as he pointed out, there was no slave state ready to come in. His words were so violent many feared that his state might again threaten to secede from the Union. But again, the soft-spoken senator from Kentucky found a way to let California come in as a free state and at the same time satisfy South Carolina.

Thinking of those slaves who had escaped, he proposed that Congress pass a law saying that all slaves found in any free state should be seized and sent back to their masters at once. *And* without trial.

WITHOUT TRIAL! exclaimed the anti-slavery people. That meant that either by mistake or on purpose any free black person who had never been a slave might also be seized and carried off. That law was too evil to be obeyed. Most people believed that whether they liked a law or not, a law was a law and had to be obeyed. So what could be done about it?

One person who thought of something she herself could do was a little lady by the name of Harriet Beecher Stowe.

Uncle Tom and little Eva

MRS. HARRIET BEECHER STOWE was a tiny person as lively as a cricket and busy as a bee. For eighteen years she had lived on the Ohio River in the town of Cincinnati. Soon after the new Slave Law was passed she was on her way home to New England, where she had been born and lived as a child. She was shocked to find that many people there knew so little about slavery that they approved of the new law. She decided she must write a book about what she had seen in Ohio and over the river in Kentucky. Her main character would be a good, kind, faithful black man called Uncle Tom.

Simon Legree

Eliza

Sitting in church one Sunday morning, she imagined Uncle Tom as an old man being beaten to death by a cruel master, and she began to sob. She wrote that last chapter first. Harriet was thrilled by the story while she was writing, but when it was done she was afraid no one would read it and it would do no good for the anti-slavery cause.

Instead it was read by thousands and as much as any other one thing helped to put an end to slavery in the United States. Within a year after it was published eight printing presses running day and night could not supply the demand for more and more copies of Mrs. Stowe's book. She had called it UNCLE TOM'S CABIN, or Life among the Lowly.

ONE SPRING DAY IN 1854, Abraham Lincoln sat in his law office in Springfield, Illinois, reading the latest news from Washington about another new law passed by Congress called the Kansas-Nebraska Act. It was a senator from Illinois, Stephen A. Douglas, who had proposed this law.

Kansas was then ready to become a state. So he had proposed that instead of Congress having to make the decision, the people living there should decide whether it should be a slave state or a free state.

No sooner was the law passed than slave owners from the south and settlers from the north went racing into Kansas to get control of the territory. Fighting between them began and was so long and so bloody that the land they were fighting over became known as "bloody Kansas."

Lincoln was sure that the same thing would happen wherever the new law was tried. How the terrible problem of slavery could finally be solved he did not know. But he did know that the United States could not go on much longer half slave and half free. Abraham Lincoln then made a decision that was to change his life.

In the summer of 1858 he challenged Senator Douglas to a series of debates on the slavery question. The complete story of these debates was printed in newspapers all over the country.

"Who is that man Lincoln out there in Illinois?" people began to ask. They wanted to hear him speak. Invitations came to him from as far away as New York City.

19

1858

By then a new Republican Party had been formed by those who wished to stop the spread of slavery. In 1860 these Republicans nominated Abraham Lincoln for President, and he was elected. So on that drizzly February morning he was leaving Springfield for Washington.

Just a week before he left, South Carolina and six other southern states had broken away from the Union and formed the Confederate States of America. Their President, Jefferson Davis of Mississippi, was proud to say:

"Our separation from the old Union is now complete."

But was it? Did those states have the right to separate from the Union? Abraham Lincoln said No. Andrew Jackson had said No thirty years ago when South Carolina had first threatened to secede. Lincoln looked back to what President Jackson had said at that time, before writing the speech he was to give on the day he was made President.

This is the Capitol Building as it looked that day. The dome was not yet finished. Soldiers stood on guard at every window as Lincoln appeared upon the platform. He spoke especially to his "countrymen" in the South, urging them not to act in haste, assuring them that there would be no war unless they started it.

Then he took the oath of office, promising as President to preserve, protect, and defend the Constitution of the United States. Would he be able to keep that solemn promise? Would he be able to restore the broken Union? That was the awful task that now rested upon Lincoln.

O NE MONTH LATER the Civil War had begun. On April 12 Fort Sumter, a United States fort off the coast of South Carolina, was fired upon and captured by South Carolina soldiers. The Stars and Stripes came down. The rebel flag went up. A wave of celebration swept through the South.

Four more states seceded—Arkansas, Tennessee, North Carolina, and Virginia—making eleven in all.

With a sad heart, Lincoln sent out a call for 75,000 volunteers to serve in the Union army for three months. Soon the soldiers came pouring into Washington, very sure they could beat the rebels in less time than that. No one could imagine then that the war would last four years.

Richmond, Virginia, had been made the capital of the Confederacy. By June the Union soldiers had crossed the Potomac River into Virginia. Their purpose was to capture Richmond.

The Confederate army, whose purpose was to capture Washington, had marched as far north as a small creek called Bull Run. There the two armies fought the first battle. It was on a Sunday in July, and Washington people drove out in carriages to view the battle as if they were going to a horse race or a ball game. From noon on, Lincoln was listening in the telegraph office of the War Department, which was just across the lawn from the White House. At first the news was good, but by six o'clock the battle was lost. Panic-stricken sightseers came tearing back into Washington, sure the rebel army was right behind them. But it was not, and Washington was safe.

April 12, 1861

THIS IS GENERAL ROBERT E. LEE on his famous
horse Traveler. Lee's home was in Arlington, Virginia,
just across the river from Washington, D.C. When Virginia
seceded he resigned from the United States Army and joined
that of Virginia, sincerely believing that he must be loyal to

his native state. During the summer of 1862 he saved Richmond from being captured.

The Union army had then landed on a strip of land between the York River and the James, known as the Peninsula. They came within ten miles of Richmond, but got no farther. General Lee had less than three fourths as many men, but he used them so well that he forced the Union army back down the Peninsula. After seven bloody battles in seven days, the Union general was obliged to admit the campaign was a failure and to leave Virginia.

R.E.Lee

HOUR AFTER HOUR, DAY AND NIGHT, Lincoln sat in the telegraph office of the War Department. His face was drawn in agony as he thought of all those boys dead on the battlefields in Virginia. The time had come to do the one thing he knew of that might still persuade the slave states to stop fighting and come back into the Union.

One day he asked the manager of the telegraph office for a piece of paper, saying that he had something special to write. Soon he called a Cabinet meeting to read what he had written. It was an announcement, or proclamation, that on the first

Abraham Lincoln

of January, 1863, the slaves would be set free in any state which was still at war with the Union. The states were given four months to reply. The four months passed.

There was no reply from any one of those eleven states that formed the Confederacy.

New Year's Day came, and with it came the annual reception in the East Room of the White House. Lincoln stood shaking hands with guests until midafternoon. Then he was told that the Secretary of State was waiting for him in his office. He had brought the final copy of the Proclamation for the President to sign—the Emancipation Proclamation.

"My hand is stiff from shaking hands all morning," said Lincoln as he took up the pen. "I hope my writing does not tremble. I would not want anyone to say that I hesitated to sign my name to this paper. For I never in all my life felt more certain that I was doing right."

This is one of the great events in American history. From then on the Civil War was fought not simply to restore the Union as it was, but to restore the Union *without slavery*—to make all of its people free.

1863

ONE OF THE WORST BATTLES in this sad war between the states took place in Pennsylvania, near the small town of Gettysburg. It was a dreadful battle lasting three days—the first three days in July, 1863. When it was over nearly 50,000 men from north and south lay dead or wounded on the battlefield. In November a ceremony was held to dedicate the battlefield as a national cemetery.

The principal speaker of the day talked for two hours. No one remembers what he said. Lincoln spoke only a few minutes, but the wonderful words of his Gettysburg Address will never be forgotten. This is part of what he said:

Four score and
seven years ago our
fathers brought forth
on this continent a
new nation . . . . . .
- - - - - - - - -
- - - - - - - - -
- - - - - . .
. .

"Fourscore and seven years ago our fathers brought forth on this continent a new nation, conceived in liberty, and dedicated to the proposition that all men are created equal.

"Now we are engaged in a great civil war, testing whether that nation, or any nation so conceived and so dedicated, can long endure. We are met on a great battlefield of that war. We have come to dedicate a portion of that field, as the final resting place for those who here gave their lives that that nation might live. . . .

"It is for us the living . . . to be here dedicated to the great task remaining before us, . . . that these dead shall not have died in vain—that this nation, under God, shall have a new birth of freedom—and that government of the people, by the people, for the people, shall not perish from the earth."

HERE IS GENERAL ULYSSES S. GRANT meeting
President Lincoln for the first time at a reception in the
White House. After he had shaken hands with Mrs. Lincoln,
everyone was so eager to see him he had to stand up on a red
satin sofa. He hated to. He was too shy. A short, stubby man
in a wrinkled uniform and dusty boots, he looked very little
like a conquering hero. But that is what he was.

30

U.S. Grant

For three years he had been fighting to gain control of the Mississippi River. He had captured the last rebel fort the day after the battle of Gettysburg. The President had then sent for him to take command of the army on the Potomac River and bring the war to an end. By that time the Confederate army had dwindled to half the size of the Union army. Its soldiers had neither enough food nor ammunition. Still they fought on desperately and bravely for another year, faithful to their great commander, General Robert E. Lee.

At last on April 9, 1865, at 4:30 P.M., Lincoln received the long-awaited telegram from General Grant at Appomattox Court House saying that General Lee had surrendered.

Next morning at dawn a 500-gun salute to victory boomed out over the Potomac River. People cheering and singing filled the White House lawn. The President appeared at an upstairs window as the band was playing *The Battle Hymn of the Republic,* the war song of the North. He asked them also to play *Dixie,* the song of the South. Then they played *The Star Spangled Banner,* the favorite anthem of what was once more the United States of America. Lincoln was happy. The awful task that had faced him four years ago had been accomplished. The Union had been saved. Even the dome of the Capitol

31

April 9, 1865

Building had now been completed. His work was done.

A few nights later he had a strange dream. He thought he heard sobbing and followed the sound to the East Room of the White House. In the center of the room he saw a coffin draped in black. He asked who was dead.

"The President," said one of the guards. "He was killed by an assassin."

"Don't worry about it," he said to Mrs. Lincoln the next morning. "God knows what is best. I think He will work this out in his own good way and time."

Friday, April 14, 1865, was Abraham Lincoln's last day. It was a lovely spring day. The air was soft and the dogwood was in blossom along the Potomac as he and Mrs. Lincoln went for a drive in the late afternoon.

That evening they went to the theatre to see a play. The President's box, close to the stage, was draped in red, white, and blue. During the third act a shot rang out. A man leaped toward the stage from the President's box. Lincoln slumped forward in his seat. All night he lay in the shadowy valley between life and death. Then he was gone. Abraham Lincoln was gone. And only then did the people of his world begin to realize how great he was.

Darwin

Part Two
WRITERS
AND
SCIENTISTS

Mark Twain

Dickens

Douglass

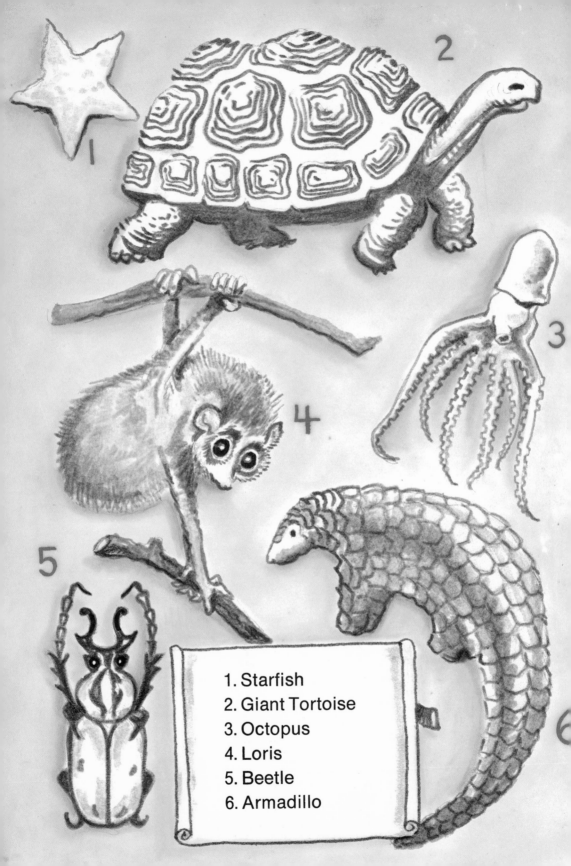

1. Starfish
2. Giant Tortoise
3. Octopus
4. Loris
5. Beetle
6. Armadillo

T HE GREAT ENGLISH SCIENTIST Charles Darwin was exactly the same age as Abraham Lincoln, born on the same day. Charles Darwin was a gentle, quiet person. In the year 1861 he was living happily with his wife and children in a country house not far from London. Every morning he could be found in his study, peering through a microscope, jotting down notes, comparing pieces of bone or examining a flower. Though he was always absorbed in his work, he was

35

Darwin

never cross or impatient when one of his boys dashed in to ask a question or to borrow his long ruler.

Charles Darwin was very unlike his own father, Dr. Darwin, who was a stern and crusty man. He was always scowling and scolding young Charles for spending so much time collecting bugs and beetles that he did not do well in school. Charles did not do well in college, either. Though he managed to graduate from Cambridge University, the only thing he really enjoyed was going on long walks with his geology professor collecting rocks and fossils.

Then came the summer of 1831 and a surprise invitation, which led to the most marvelous adventure of Darwin's entire life. He was asked to go as a natural scientist on the *Beagle,* a ship being sent out by the British government to survey the west coast of South America, visit the South Sea Islands, and return by way of the Indian Ocean. This voyage took five years.

One of the most interesting places Darwin visited was the Galapagos Islands, about 500 miles west of South America. There he saw giant tortoises and other primitive animals found nowhere else. And yet they differed from island to island. Why was that? he wondered.

Then the great idea dawned on him: From the beginning

of time, animals must have been developing naturally whatever they needed to survive—thicker fur, longer necks, sharper claws, whatever it was. Those who could not do this died off. Those who could passed on the necessary characteristic to the next generation, until it became permanent and a new species was formed. This was a new idea. Darwin realized that it would shock many people who had been taught to believe that all the animals that ever were or would be had come walking two by two out of Noah's Ark. So he kept on collecting proofs for twenty years, until 1859. Then he finally published what he had discovered in a book called

ON THE ORIGIN OF SPECIES

As he expected, he was both ridiculed and attacked, just as Galileo had been when he announced that the earth revolved around the sun. A friend of Darwin, who was a philosopher, said that had been the fate of every great discovery.

"First people say, 'It is ridiculous.' Then they say, 'It is contrary to the Bible.' And then they say, 'We always knew that it was true.' "

Charles Darwin quietly endured what could not be helped and went on every morning as usual with his work. Within twenty years he was to see his ideas widely accepted.

David Copperfield

IT WAS THE NIGHT OF DECEMBER 2, 1861, in Edin-
burgh, Scotland. The lights in the hall were dimmed. The
audience was quiet. All eyes were focused on the stage as a
man in the spotlight began to read the opening words of *A
Christmas Carol*. The man reading them was Charles Dickens,
the author himself. Dickens was on a tour of Scotland, Ire-

land, and England, reading from his books *Oliver Twist, David Copperfield,* and others, as well as from the Christmas story of old Scrooge and Tiny Tim. The readings were an enormous success. Often when he finished, he said, "The audience would not go, but sat applauding like mad."

One night in another city, too many tickets had been sold in advance. Dickens described what happened as hundreds came crowding into a place already full.

"I read with the platform crammed with people. I got them to lie down upon it. One pretty girl in full dress lying on her side all night holding onto the legs of my table. It was a most extraordinary sight. And yet from the moment I began to read they never missed a point and ended with a burst of cheers."

39

Dickens finished his tour in London, where he said the money returns were astounding. An agent from Australia was there offering a large sum of money for an eight-months tour of his country. Dickens was tempted, but, since he was not very well, the thought of the long sea voyage to Australia kept him from accepting.

Dickens had visited the United States in 1842. Now, the Civil War kept him from returning. Two years after the war ended, he sailed to America, and on December 2, 1867, he gave his first reading in Boston. An immense line of people waited in the freezing street for twelve hours to buy tickets.

In New York City five thousand people stood in two lines three-quarters of a mile long. Speculators were offering twenty dollars apiece for anyone's place in line. But no one would take it.

Dickens also gave performances in Philadelphia, Baltimore, and Washington before returning to England. The *Christmas Carol* was one of his favorite readings, the one he gave most often. The first reading from his books that Dickens ever gave was from *Christmas Carol*. That was a benefit performance in April, 1857, in London, to help build and furnish a new hospital for children.

W HO IN THE YEAR 1861 had ever read *The Adventures of Tom Sawyer* or heard of Huckleberry Finn? Nobody. Who had ever heard of an author named Mark Twain? Nobody. Samuel L. Clemens, the man who was to use that name, was then a pilot on a Mississippi River steamboat. "Mark twain" was an expression that any pilot

41

Mark Twain

was happy to hear. It meant that the river ahead was two fathoms deep (twelve feet), so it was safe to go on.

Always as a boy, Sam had had his heart set on becoming a pilot. The small town of Hannibal, Missouri, where he grew up, was on the Mississippi River. All the boys he knew felt as he did about the big river and the steamboats that were always passing by. One day when he was nine, Sam swam across the Mississippi to the Illinois shore and back without stopping, a distance of two miles. There were so many outdoor things to do Sam never liked to be in school. After he was twelve, he didn't have to be. That was in 1847. That year his father died and Sam persuaded his mother to let him go to work for a printer. He learned so fast that within a year he could set type and run a small press. Seven years later he was still working as a printer when luck came his way.

One cold winter night as he was on his way home, a bit of paper went whirling past him in the wind and lodged against a wall. It was a fifty-dollar bill—more money than Sam had ever seen! No one claimed it, so with that fifty dollars he bought a ticket to Cincinnati, and from there he took a steamboat down to New Orleans. At first the old ship's pilot did not want to teach him to steer the boat, but finally agreed to, and

42

he said later: "Within a year and a half from the time he came on the river, Sam was not only a pilot but a good one."

Four years later the Civil War broke out and Samuel Clemens went north on the last steamboat to make the trip from New Orleans to St. Louis. After that all regular river traffic was stopped. Steamboats would not be running again on the Mississippi until after General Grant had captured the last Confederate fort, at Vicksburg.

Luckily in 1861 Sam's oldest brother had just been made Secretary of the Territory of Nevada. Sam went with him. In the overland stage coach, drawn by sixteen galloping horses, they made the trip in nineteen days from St. Louis, Missouri, to Carson City, Nevada. Carson City was the capital of the territory. Sam began writing reports about the legislature for the weekly newspaper. Soon his stories and articles were being copied up and down the West Coast. One day he told the editor that he would like to sign his name to them, saying:

"I want to sign them 'Mark Twain.' It is an old river term always pleasant for a pilot to hear, meaning safe waters."

The new name appeared for the first time on Sunday, February 2, 1863. That is how and when the pilot Samuel L. Clemens became the author Mark Twain.

THIS IS FREDDY BAILEY, a small slave boy born in eastern Maryland, who remained a slave until he was twenty-one. In spite of that poor start he was to become a famous man: Frederick Douglass, speaker, editor, friend of President Lincoln, and later United States ambassador to Haiti.

Freddy never knew who his father was. His mother, Harriet Bailey, died when he was very young. He had never seen her by daylight. She had been sent away soon after he was born to work in the fields of another plantation. To see him, she had to walk twelve miles each way after dark and be back at work again before sunrise or be whipped.

Aunt Katy, an old slave woman, took charge of the small children until they were old enough to work. She was ugly and irritable and often did not give them enough to eat. Many times they waited to get "crumbs and small bones flung out for the dogs and cats." When he was eight, Freddy Bailey was put to work amusing and chasing after the small son of his master. The baby boy's mother began teaching Freddy the alphabet until her husband found it out and made her stop.

"Don't you know," he said, "it's bad business to teach a slave to read? As soon as they can read, slaves get discontented and are no longer any good."

Freddy heard what was said. In time, by watching and listening and trying, he taught himself to read and write.

The more he read, the more discontented he became and the more determined to be free. But how? To run away was a difficult and dangerous thing to try. Years went by. He was working at the shipyards in Baltimore when he managed to escape. Disguised in a uniform borrowed from a sailor, he slipped onto a train, got to New York City, and from there went on to Massachusetts. To be safe he then changed his name to Frederick Douglass.

The year was 1838. The great anti-slavery movement had

begun in the North. Douglass became one of its most eloquent speakers. He also published an anti-slavery newspaper. When the Civil War began he recruited black soldiers for the Union army. Their pay was not equal to that of white soldiers, so he went to call on President Lincoln. He was cordially received and well pleased by the meeting.

On March 4, 1865, Abraham Lincoln became President for the second time. That evening Frederick Douglass attended the reception in the White House. He tells what happened in his *Autobiography*. Since he was the only black man waiting in line to enter the White House door, he was stopped by the police, until Lincoln received word that he was there. Then said Douglass:

"It was not long before I walked into the spacious East Room. Like a mountain pine high above all the others, Mr. Lincoln stood in his grand simplicity and homely beauty. Even before I reached him, he exclaimed, 'Here comes my friend Douglass.' Taking me by the hand he said, 'I am glad to see you. I saw you in the crowd today, listening to my inaugural address. How did you like it?' I replied, 'Mr. Lincoln, that was a sacred effort.' 'I am glad,' he said. 'There is no man in the country whose opinion I value more than yours.' "

Victoria

Tzu Hsi

Part Three

AROUND
THE WORLD

Mutsuhito

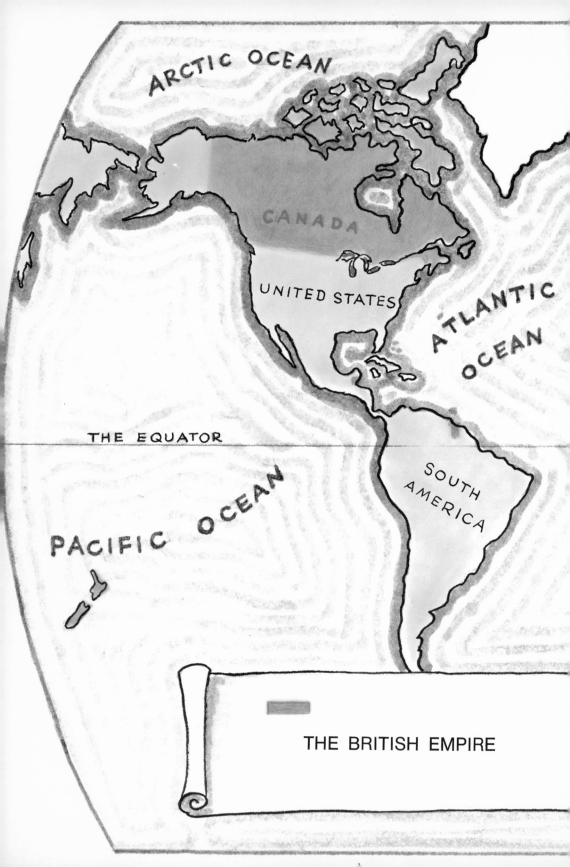

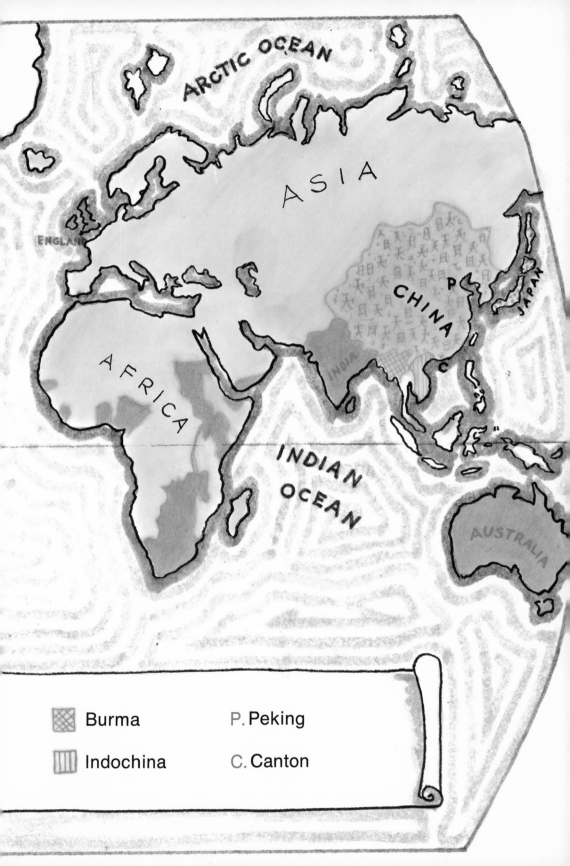

ARCTIC OCEAN

ASIA

ENGLAND

CHINA

P

JAPAN

C

INDIA

AFRICA

INDIAN
OCEAN

AUSTRALIA

Burma

P. Peking

Indochina

C. Canton

QUEEN VICTORIA was queen of England when Lincoln was President. In 1861 she had been queen for twenty-four years and was to rule for another forty years, mak-

England

ing hers the longest reign of any king or queen in English history. It was also one of the best.

From the time she was a little girl, Victoria kept a diary and wrote in it faithfully every night before she went to bed. Then as she knelt to say her prayers she always included her uncle the King, asking God to bless him.

Victoria was eleven before she was actually told that, since her father was dead, she would one day be queen. It was such a terrifying thought, she felt like crying.

"I will be good," she said as bravely as she could. But that night she sobbed herself to sleep.

Before daybreak, one month after her eighteenth birthday, her uncle the King died. This is what Victoria wrote in her diary at the end of that day, Tuesday, June 20, 1837:

"I was awoke at 6 o'clock by Mamma, who told me that the Archbishop of Canterbury and Lord C . . . were here and wished to see me. I got out of bed and went into my sitting room (only in my dressing gown) and saw them. Lord C then acquainted me that my poor Uncle the King had expired at 12 minutes past 2 this morning and consequently that I am Queen. I am very young but I am sure that very few have a more real desire to do what is right than I have."

Three years later, in 1840, the queen married her handsome German cousin Albert, who was as good as he was handsome. They left London after the ceremony for a three day honeymoon at Windsor Castle. From there Victoria wrote a letter bubbling with joy to her Uncle Leopold in Belgium:

"I write you from here, the happiest happiest Being that ever existed. Albert is an Angel . . . What I can do to make him happy will be my greatest delight. . . ."

Victoria and Albert became the proud and happy parents of nine children. Here is the royal family in 1857 when the last baby was born. The tall boy on the right is the future king, Edward VII, the great-grandfather of the present Queen Elizabeth.

Prince Albert did all that he could to help Victoria with her many duties as queen. Every day he was up early and put in long hours of work. He read all of the day's newspapers, greatly concerned about affairs in Europe, as well as in England. He wanted most of all to promote peace and understanding among nations. His last act was to prevent war with the United States.

In 1861, when Civil War began in America, England was determined to remain neutral. But in November the captain

of a United States warship made the mistake of boarding an English mail ship. This so infuriated many Englishmen that they were ready to declare war. An angry message was prepared by the foreign ministers and sent to Windsor Castle for the Queen to sign. Prince Albert read it first and saw that it should not be sent. Though he was ill, he sat down by his green-shaded lamp and spent all night going over it, smoothing out every sentence that might irritate the United States. By eight o'clock he had it ready to show the queen. But by then he had a high fever and soon became so ill that the doctors could not save his life. He died just four days before his message reached the White House. It was a courteous request to acknowledge that the American captain had made a mistake, which President Lincoln was willing to do.

Christmas, 1861, was a sad day for Queen Victoria, desolate and heartbroken without Albert. From then on she told ministers she would be guided only by what Albert would have wished. She did not make the laws. The laws were made by Parliament. The Prime Minister and other ministers made plans and policies, but they consulted the queen. And those sixty-four years during which she gave her opinion are known as the Victorian Era.

During those years the British Empire reached the peak of its prosperity and power. Year by year more and more lands were conquered, until England ruled one fifth of the entire surface of the globe.

But whatever land England acquired, another nation or tribe of people had to lose. That is the way, since the beginning of history, all empires have been created.

THE OLDEST EMPIRE in the world at this time was the ancient Empire of China, which was over 3,000 years old and set in its ancient ways of living and thinking.

55

China

Although the world had changed, all people outside of its borders were still looked upon as "barbarians."

In the summer of 1861 a five-year-old boy became the emperor of China, but the real ruler of that proud and ancient empire was his mother, the Empress Tzu Hsi.

Unlike Queen Victoria, who ruled the British Empire at the same time, Tzu Hsi was not born into the royal family. She had gained her power through her cleverness and charm. In 1850, when she was fifteen, she had been one of the new wives selected for the emperor. Though she started in the lowest rank, she so enchanted the emperor that he soon raised her position to that of second wife. And when Tzu Hsi gave the emperor his first son, she rose even higher in his favor. Before long she began to offer him advice about running the empire, which he, being too lazy to think much about it himself, usually accepted.

First of all, Tzu Hsi insisted that the ancient ban against foreigners should never be set aside. Never had any foreign ambassador been allowed to enter the sacred city of Peking except to pay tribute to the emperor. Even though the new barbarian nations from the West were clamoring to have this honorable custom set aside, it must never be done.

Two of those barbarian nations from the West were England and France. They resented being called barbarians. They were determined to have their ambassadors allowed to live in Peking. So in 1856 they joined together and made war upon China. Cannons from their ships "roared like a million thunderclaps" over the city of Canton.

What else could the Chinese do but sue for peace? They had no cannon, no rifles, only ancient weapons useful in hand-to-hand fighting. Even so, the English ambassadors who went to sign the peace treaty were not allowed to enter Peking. At the summer palace south of the city, they were seized and mistreated by the guards. At that the English general marched north in a rage and had that most beautiful summer palace of the emperor burned to the ground.

The emperor was not there. As the English army drew near he had fled to another palace at Jehol, taking all the imperial family with him, except one brother. This prince was left behind to face that shameful day when the foreign ambassadors had to be admitted to Peking.

First to arrive was the British ambassador. Crowds of curious Chinese people lined the way eager to see the "Great Barbarian" as he was carried in a palanquin to a gold and scarlet pavilion where the prince was waiting.

The treaty which China was forced to sign was very costly. Burma, which had paid tribute to China for six hundred years, had to be handed over to England. Indochina went to France. There were many other humiliating demands.

Very soon in the palace at Jehol, death came to the emperor. And in the summer of 1861, the new five-year-old emperor returned to Peking with his mother, the Empress Tzu Hsi, who was then in great danger. Princes envious of her power over the small boy schemed and plotted to be rid of her. One wrong word of hers would have meant instant death. But she made no such mistake. She, too, was a schemer. Year by year she gathered more and more power until in 1908, when she died, that utterly selfish but still charming old lady was the absolute ruler of the empire. Almost everyone called her the "old Buddha."

During all of these years China continued to be attacked on all sides, insulted, weakened, shattered, and torn apart from within and without by wars and rebellion. Trapped in its ancient ways, the empire was helpless to defend itself, and, as a form of government, it lasted only three years after the old empress was gone.

JAPAN'S MEETING with the nations from the west was very different from that of China. For over two hundred years Japan had been cut off completely from the outside world. No Japanese person had been allowed to leave the country, no foreigner allowed to enter it.

Then, in July, 1853, an American, Commodore Matthew C. Perry, visited Japan and early the next year persuaded one of the high officials to sign a treaty of friendship with the United States. Later a trade agreement was also signed by the prime minister of Japan. When certain lords objected to this change, he pointed to what had happened in China, saying, "If we, too, persist in clinging to our old ways, Heaven knows what worse calamity may befall our Empire."

In 1860 the first delegation of Japanese gentlemen left for the United States to bring back a report of what the outer world was like. One of them kept a diary from which these few sentences are copied:

"Apr. 28. We are going to the home of the ruler this

morning. We are putting on our finest kimono. The ruler
of this country is called President. There is no policeman in
the President's house and no fortress in his yard. It is very
beautiful but different from what we expected.

"In Washington and all other American cities the mothers
do not carry their babies on their backs [as they do in Japan]
but in small carriages. . . .

60

"May 21. There is a telegraph line between New York and Philadelphia over which messages are sent as fast as lightning, but I cannot describe it.

"June 9. [They were in New York City and visited the home of Commodore Perry.] The home was very fine and decorated with many Japanese mementos. We were entertained with cake and wine. Two Japanese spaniels sniffed our clothes, leaped in our laps and were so affectionate that we were quite sad for them and shed a tear when we left."

On July 13th they sailed for home. There they found that the prime minister had been assassinated and a civil war was raging between those who did and those who did not approve of the changes taking place. The start which Japan had made might have been blocked if it had not been for the remarkable young Prince Mutsuhito, who, earlier that year, had been declared heir to the throne.

Seven years later, when he was fifteen, Mutsuhito became emperor. He began at once to make his reign worthy to be called *meiji,* meaning "enlightened government." He made and kept a solemn promise to "seek knowledge throughout the world." Soon western ideas and inventions came pouring into Japan. Railroads were built; a telegraph system set up; national banks and a postoffice founded; ships were built for a navy and an army was equipped with modern weapons. Newspapers, schools, and colleges came into being. Never in the history of the world had so many changes taken place so fast as they did during the enlightened reign of the great Mutsuhito, who became emperor of Japan just two years after the death of Abraham Lincoln.

INDEX

Numbers in italics refer to maps

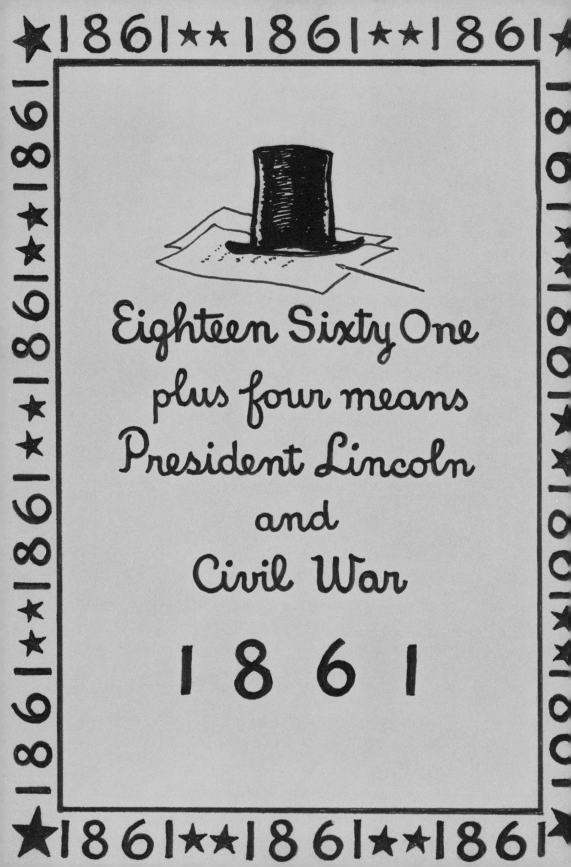

Eighteen Sixty One
plus four means
President Lincoln
and
Civil War

1861